SOAR IN YOUR SORROWS

Paradise's Storm

MCCLURE PUBLISHING, INC.

Cover Design by Kathy McClure

To order additional copies, please contact:
McClure Publishing, Inc.
www.mcclurepublishing.com
800-659-4908

Table of Contents

INTRODUCTION

ODE TO MOTHER NATURE

ODE TO PATRICE

ODE TO MY READERS

James 1:2-3 "Consider it pure joy, whenever you face trials of many kinds because you know that the testing of your faith produce perseverance." (NIV)

The Poetry Of Me

Versatile this woman is
Everything, this woman can be
Never limited to one ability
Never limited to what the eye can see
Beauty in the versatility of me
I'm in love with the poetry I can be

The journey is not a destination,
but a lifelong adventure.
Pray to be led down the right path
every day.

SOAR IN YOUR SORROWS
FLOW IN YOUR BLESSINGS.

INTRODUCTION

The poems written in this book are an artistic expression of feelings. These poems were written during Patrice's healing journey. The poems written in this book take you from a state of over-thinking to a state of self-love and of lighter consciousness.

Patrice is owner of the brand, Modernly Ethnic (M.E.), embodies the modern-day individual. Modernly Ethnic is a bridge between healing and creativity. M.E.'s motto is, "love who you are, express who are you, be who you are." M.E.'s three main aims are self-love, self-care, and creativity. M.E. spotlights the whole you, physically, mentally, emotionally, and spiritually.

Along Patrice's journey, she authored many self-love affirmations that you will see in later published material. Patrice wrote her first set of affirmations in the face of her own heart break and adversity. These affirmations can be found on Modernly Ethnic's YouTube Channel. Engaging in this helped elevate her own undesirable feelings to comfort, peace, joy, and experiencing heaven on earth. Patrice hopes that these affirmations will help you to do the same.

Heaven on earth is an optimistic state of mind that is achievable. The opposite of the feeling of heaven on earth is mental turmoil. Mental turmoil is a state of mind that eats away at your joy and happiness; it's a pessimistic voice replaying over and over in your head that you listen to and allow to be there. Taking control of this voice is examining it and telling it no, you don't belong to me. Doing this at first will be hard, it may feel forced, until it becomes a natural habit that you will be grateful for forever more.

We hope that you join Modernly Ethnic, The Creative Community, on this journey of self-love, self-care, and healing, through a higher state of consciousness to your creative self. The Creative Community is where all creative people come together for support and praise. You are welcomed to share your creative endeavors by emailing Patrice at modernlyethnic@gmail.com, for a chance to be featured on Modernly Ethnic's blog.

We are on Facebook, Instagram, Twitter, and YouTube at "modernlyethnic". Modernly Ethnic owns two websites, www.modernlyethnic.org and www.modernlyethnic.blogspot.com. Our Blogspot site is where Modernly Ethnic was birthed and our ".org" site is what Modernly Ethnic has grown into. There is much more to come from Patrice and Modernly Ethnic so stay tuned.

Self-love Tips

Use your weaknesses

to make you strong and gentle

because there's beauty in all things.

~~~

Never tell anyone how to love you.

~~~

Don't isolate yourself and don't make things worse than

what they are.

~~~

Self-love is about aligning your heart, mind, body, and spirit.

~~~

Your thoughts have the power to change your life for better or worst.

~~~

Along your journey of self-love, your mind will begin to change from what you've been conditioned to believe.

~~~

The truth of love is when one's words lines up with their actions.

~~~

As humans, we are complex individuals. Only make decisions when your head and heart are aligned, not when you are angry. Don't let any emotion make your decisions.

~~~

Self-love is about finding things within you that you love, not waiting for the validation or confirmation from others.

~~~

Self-love is discovering yourself and learning from your lessons.

~~~

Its human nature for our minds to go to the negative, but when you work hard to acknowledge, feel, evaluate, and let go of negative thoughts, you can live the life you want with ease and a healthier mind. Your thoughts don't make you who you are, your actions do.

~~~

Be comfortable with all your emotions, even the bad ones. Repression of your emotions may result in physical pain and depression. Your emotions are temporary and are meant to be felt. Keep in mind, your emotions are there to teach you lessons and enhance your life.

~~~

Don't be comfortable giving others power over you. Letting someone have power over you means allowing them to make you feel low within yourself.

~~~

Not everything and everyone can go with you on your journey.

~~~

It's okay getting upset at someone for valid reasons but to wallow in your sorrows or feeling like your life is over is not only wrong, but unhealthy. If this happens, work your hardest to never give them that power again.
Do this by learning who you are
and loving yourself unconditionally.

~~~

Only seek self-validation,

self-approval,

and self-satisfaction.

~~~

Use your negative emotions as tools to grow.

~~~

Just because you love someone

doesn't mean you have to put up with a behavior that

doesn't align with your soul or spirit.

~~~

Protect yourself.

Stand your ground.

Set boundaries and stick to them.

~~~

Detach yourself from temporary satisfactions.

You are built for greatness.

Work for what you want, in all things.

~~~

Here's to gently improving yourself every day for the rest of your life.

~~~

Message to Readers:

If this poetry helps you face your feelings

The feelings that lies deep inside

The feelings you try to hide

I will be grateful

My soul blessed

My purpose fulfilled

Poetry

Reality is what I get to say in real life

Poetry is what I feel in my soul

Poetry is my scars written down

Poetry sets me free

Lust

Can't have love without pain
Can't have sunshine without the rain
People want love but don't trust
People want to be in love but instead *lust*

Contradicting Things

They tell us not to live in the past but to hold on to our
memories

They tell us that pain is bad but there's no life without pain

They tell us that love isn't supposed to hurt but the ones we
love hurt us the most

They lie not to hurt us but it in fact does

Our minds are full of *contradicting things*

Needing Balance

Sometimes I imagine myself 20 years from now, wondering
the state of mind I'll be in or what I would have
accomplished.
I mostly imagine how I would feel after being on this earth
for so long.
I understand now that life is full of pain and that's mostly
because it needs balance.
You can't have love without pain
or have sunshine without rain.

Goodness

Goodness in the darkest time
Goodness where the sun doesn't shine
Goodness when everything is shit
Goodness, why can't I get enough of
it?

Joy when you are hopeless
Joy in the unhappiest situations
Joy, where are you hiding?
Joy, please come and find me

Balance

What's life without *balance*?

Ups and downs

Triumphs and trials

Through it all

You must remain balanced too

Like what makes you, you

Stick to that

Remain humble, but brag from time to time

Tell yourself how much of the shit you are

But also, tell yourself when you're wrong

Forgiveness

Feel. Heal. Secure.

Feel secure enough to *heal* yourself

Seek the higher power from above

Feel the love

The hug

You can just ask for and receive

No matter how bad it is, He forgives thee

So forgive yourself

Forgive him

Forgive her

Forgive them all

Forgive them all so you can *heal* properly

Forgive yourself so you can grow

Broken Heart

Sometimes I awake with your smell and I hate it

Memories of you make me feel sedated

Like I am walking dead

I wish I could rip them all into shreds

But unfortunately, memories don't work this way

They linger on until we've had enough of them

But it doesn't help that you won't leave me alone

It doesn't help that people want to see us together again

After what you did to me

After the lies you told

The pain you caused

I just want to let it go

Forever a *broken-hearted girl*

Love is Born

The stars cannot shine without the darkness

Yeah, shit might be fucked up right now

But what's life without balance

What's light without darkness

What's hope without hopelessness

Yeah, you might be vulnerable and a little open

But I promise you'll get through it and blossom

There's always a light at the end of the tunnel

If you stop now, you'll never see it

Giving up before you can even be it

Be all you were meant

to be

Be the rainbow after

the storm

Because through pain,

love is born

Being Selfish

Being selfish means a lot
It means looking to yourself for everything
That includes your problems and
Your triumphs
The days you need self-care
The days, the hours, the minutes, the seconds
you take to think about yourself
The things you do to show yourself you love you
The things you think and do that will help you be better

The things you do to work on yourself

That shower

That face mask

All those encouraging
words you tell yourself

All those good things
you say about yourself
and mean

All the things that
people don't see

That's why being
selfish is alright with
me

Hopeless Love

I thought we might have

been meant to be

But I'm done thinking

of love so childishly

Done thinking of you

and me hopelessly in love

Remembering who we were before

Before the world became a real thing

Before the fear of dying even meant anything

Before the lettering of our names, you and me

on that tree disappeared to nothing

I thought we might have been meant to be

But I'm done thinking of love so childishly

Childishly hopeful for happily ever after

Childishly wishing this love was the real thing

Unimaginable Feelings

That feeling you feel after you've done something new
or seen something you never saw
That feeling when your mind, body, and spirit all align
In that very moment to not miss the beauty of it
All the pain, anger, and sadness seems to float away

The realization that even while in pain you can feel happiness
and joy
Even with heartache,
something else has the ability to satisfy you
For instance, the feeling of reaching your goals
feels undeniably beautiful
The acceptance that you're different and nowhere near
perfect but that's okay
The love you have for yourself is unreal
The love that *unimaginably* defines YOU

Illusion of Love

People really be out here insecure and jealous of their mates
In feeling like they don't meet up, they cheat
Not understanding they were given a chance for a reason
For their potential
Which is the biggest mistake I ever made

Mistaking an illusion for reality
An illusion of love and what we could be
But you don't get it, so you ruin it all
The illusion is over, and you're devastated
Me too
because you thought you love me
But that was an illusion too

What is love

Is it just pain

It is a rose with thorns

Lots of them

So many thorns you can barely enjoy the beauty of the Rose

Is that what we put up with for love

Thorns that pokes us constantly

Pain that never goes away

Is that what love is

Is love pain?

I'm confused

is it an illusion or is it true

Love, a drug that we can't seem to get enough of

Are we all addicts of "love" or the illusion of it

I can't

I won't

wake up from it

Heart on Sleeve

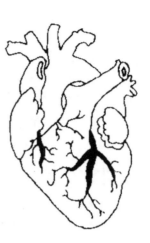

I used to wear my heart on my

sleeve

Now my big heart is incased in a

steal cage

Under lock and key

With a guard dog

That bites

That growls

That howls

Before I cried my eyes out
Cried until I was numb
When I cry now,
Those tears feel like they're drying up
I've cried my last tears for months,
years, decades, centuries
I'm hurt but I had enough

I've built up a wall but kept the door cracked
The last drop of tears acted as glue and sealed that crack
Wondering if anyone will ever feel the warm love
I know is in my heart

Depression

Depression, the black sheep of things that can have an effect on us

The dark thing we're embarrassed to admit we're going through

The thing we try our best to let go of

But *depression* is the hardest thing to climb out of

The thing that waits until you're just fine and then pulls at your foot

The thing you should kick in the face and move on with your day, your life

Which is easier said than done

But still, I'm right

It's time for us to fight

The fight most of us don't even realize we're fighting

But the moment you realize depression is a dark monster that

wants to hold you back,

you are on the right foot

Sooner or later, you'll be not easily shook

Focus on releasing instead of thinking about the pain

Focus on the sunshine after the rain

Focus on the light at the end of the tunnel,

because it's there

Staring you right in the face

But you can't handle the brightness

The brightness of better days right now

And that's okay

You just need to find a little faith
Arm yourself with it
Arm yourself with some hope too
Because faith and hope gets us
through

Lost Minds

One certain thought
Turns into another uncertain thought
The minute you think you understand
Your thoughts change

Change that we fear
Memories we hold dear to our hearts
Afraid to lose, afraid to let go of
Memories that wouldn't exist if we didn't know

Thoughts that we have in the dark
Do we ignore them or give them life
Questions we ask ourselves
Answers we never believe

Dreams that never come true
Dreams that do
Nightmares that haunt us
Replaying our unconscious thoughts

Thoughts that we ignore
Thoughts that we write down
Thoughts that make us smile
Thoughts that make us frown

Thoughts that wouldn't exist if we didn't think them
A mind that wonders but never finds

…A mind that is fine even if it's never found
Lost Minds

Tell 'Em

Don't tell me you love me then disappear on me

The first thing I'm gonna think is you phony

And imma shut down on ya

And you gonna be mad

Trynna get me back being sad

But I might be gone

you might not be able to use me for long

Use me whatever way you want

Acting like you loved me, but it was all a front

I know what you want

But I don't have that for you

I let you know that

So is that why you're really mad

You can't put up with a few months of being dry

Laughing my fucking ass off

That's a shame

Because I was really gonna try with you mane

Oh well, that's the reason I said try

Nobody is

gonna get my

hopes up just

to let them

die

Opposites

Opposites match

Opposites attract

Is the goal to find someone different

Different from what or who

Different from me

Different from you

I'm confused because I thought you were the opposite of
everything I didn't want

Turned out I just ran into the arms of the complete opposite
of you, not better

Being vulnerable is very, very dangerous

Being vulnerable will blind you from a mile away

Stay woke people

Improve yourself daily

Because its people out here priding themselves on being

shady

Sorry to sound so jaded

But I'm mad

Mad that you can trust none of what you hear

and half of what you see

But don't worry because I'm improving my intuition daily

I don't act on everything I see but I peep

Keep doing what you're doing

We all gotta keep it moving

Some of us are just learning lessons

Don't disrespect the process

Soar in your sorrows

There's always tomorrow…

One Day, Forreal

How can I ignore

What you did to me

What you let happen

How much I let you in

How close I let you get

to me

To my heart

To my spirit

To my life

Now all I do is fight

Fight myself because I love you

And I hate it

I hate expressing myself

I hate that we ever dated

But one day I'll get over you

I'll get over the fact I still love you

One day, I'll move on for real

Paranoia

Last night

I suffered from *paranoia*

Thinking all the people I wanted around were ghost

That they only existed in my mind

That my relationship was blind

Blind to the naked eye

Only real in my head

And in my heart

But in reality I was dying

For a fresh start

Felt like I should let my pain take me over

So I can force myself to find a way out

So the dreams can never come true

Dreams of wanting you

Being with you

Arguing with you

In love with you

Every day

Every night

Never ever going to sleep angry
Because we can make up
But we can't do that because we aren't together
And it's starting to rub me the wrong way
That you're not available when I need you
Why can't it all be so simple

If you don't wanna deal with me, don't
This is it
This is me
As ugly as I'll ever be
Because it don't get no worse than this
I'm a complete hot mess
I admit
Can't wait 'til I get over it

Darkness

Climb out of the darkness into
the light
Sometimes the light will find
you
Other times, you would have
to find it
It won't just be staring you right in the face
I'm sure it did that too many times before
You merely didn't appreciate it
All you knew is that it made sense
You didn't think about what you would do if the light wasn't
there
If the dark cloud came over you
Consumed you
Controlled you

But the dark cloud is just there
Eating away at your joy, your very life
It's fighting you but you're not fighting it
You're comfortable with just letting it sit
Like it's supposed to be there
Like it's a part you

Well I'm here to tell you now, it's not cool
You have a life to live
Or your life will outlive you
We're all here for a reason
Too many people think we're living to die
But we're living to live

Hiding

Hiding behind "Perfect Patty"

Always dealing

Always healing

Should I be blamed for writing my thoughts down in a

journal and dealing with my shit on my own

Should I be blamed because my problems seems less worse

than yours

I'm not even sure what this poem is even saying

Maybe this poem helps with this headache

Maybe this poem tells me more about myself

Maybe this poem shows me how all over the place

I really am

How I don't have it together at all
How I've been hiding being my healing practices
Acting like nothing fazes me
Acting like your words mean nothing

Well sometimes they do
Sometimes I hold back things I want to say
To avoid conflict, arguments, unnecessary drama
You know, deal with things in the mature, adult way
Just wanting peace in my life
No worry no stress
No stress no worry

As my mind wonders I can't help but to reminisce about all
the dumb things I worry about

Like eating

Is food really that important

Like it being your main focus three times a day

Hunger is a bitch though

A real mean one

What I'm saying is

I have to eat

Everyone has to eat

But I mean like I want my life full of things that distract me
from eating
That makes me so happy and bliss
I don't want to eat and hibernate
I want to live and celebrate

I guess things are easier said than done
Like there are a lot of factors that affect us right
Like where you live
Who your family is
The people we have no choice to be around
What our biggest childhood trauma is
The things we went through we don't even remember
The things we don't share

The way I drown myself in others' problems

All because I'm an Empath?!

All because I feel other people's emotions like they're my own

'W.t.f' a/k/a What the fuck?

Am I just bored?

I think I'm just bored

But it's real I tell you

I can feel the way others feel

I just need something to distract me

I like that my mind is racing like this

Maybe I'll try to make things more exciting

Like actually make real relationships with people

Like going back to my therapist

because I know exactly why I left

We leave therapy when we feel things are okay right

No, we leave therapy when we're making a dumb ass choice

and we don't want to be told we're wrong

Well, it's true

Even as adults we make mistakes

We may do the wrong thing sometimes

We don't know it all

No one does

That's why when people tell you
"Life is one big, long lesson"
They actually really fucking mean it
I tell myself everything happens for a reason
because I know it truly does
But is this a mere excuse, something my parents would have
told me as a child to help me cope with a fucked-up decision
I made
I guess that doesn't take away from the fact that it's
absolutely true

What's the absolute truth and what our parents should have
told us is
"Trust yourself. Love yourself"
"Whatever you did, whatever you're going through will pass"

Mental health is the beginning of it all and it ends with
self-love
It sounds simple but it's not
A lot of us don't have those two things
mental health and self-love

But I pray the world finds it

I pray I find it and never ever let it go

Unhealed Trauma

I've disconnected myself
from feeling,
If not disconnected, I've
learned to have a bit of
emotional control
Because emotions are going
to come
Do we allow them to drive us?
No, we drive them.
We use our emotions to our advantage

How can someone give their last like it's nothing?

Trying hard not to end up with nothing

but most times, that's the way it happens

Watching this has left me running,

afraid to end up feeling like I have nothing

I'll settle down one day for good

With someone I'm truly supposed to end up with

I'll be truly happy and in bliss

I would never have to question it

I would never be afraid

I would never fear losing that person

Because

THAT PERSON is ME

THAT PERSON is GOD

THAT PERSON will never ever leave my side

I'll never be lost

That's what I believe now

I wonder if it took me too long to get this down

I just look back and wonder if I left someone out of fear or

simply because they weren't the ones for me

Can't go back now

Only forward

Only controlling what I can

Only accepting what I should

Exhibiting worth, value, moral, truth

In life you're supposed to hold on to the GOOD

Instead, we just hold on to all the bad things

Instead, I just hold all the bad things in

Then explode

I think it's a problem

But I taught myself to look on the brighter side of things

The positives in life

The happies

That's how I was able to withstand the ugliest

How do you see the good in yourself if you haven't had any
practice at all
I've seen beauty in the ugliest things
I showed love regardless of anything
Before at least
Before this shit start fucking with me

While I've been running, I've been running right towards my
ultimate fate that I so "feared"
I'm changing and I mean right now, already
I'm getting inpatient
With myself
With a lotta shit
I don't mean to rush anything but I'm literally growing right
now
As we speak
As you read......
Grow with me or get the fuck on…

Flame | *Tread Lightly*

The flame dances and I feel it in my soul

First, I wonder why it dances so freely

Why doesn't it just stay still

But the flame is full of energy

It reminds me of the energy that burns within me

Dancing any which way, whichever way it feels

Not waiting for answers to unanswered questions

Not giving a damn where it goes

Going wherever the wind blows

Fire is beautiful

Flame so pretty and red, and yellow, and gold

A flame can be dangerous if used for unintended purposes

A flame can be dangerous when used for unintentional reasons

I repeat this because you might want to be careful

Tread very *lightly* around this beautiful *flame* in my soul

I'm trying my very best not to let it go

It belongs there, dancing freely, warming my bones

Fire reminds me of love

Up and down, left, and right dancing whatever way

It even sometimes goes away but can always be lit again

The flame lives to love another day

Picture the energy a flame holds

A flame can calm you but if used for unintended purposes

can harm you

Tread lightly…

Blank Canvas

Sometimes you may see the world in gray

Where everything and everyone glooms, even you

Not one flower in bloom

Don't take this so bad

Just find crayons and color your world

This is a chance to start something great

Let go of the hurt, let go of the pain

Color until the entire gray goes away

Sometimes things start out that way

A *blank* space

Waiting to be filled with whatever you choose

Plant what you want and watch it bloom

Create the reality you want to see

Be everything that you can be

Because what's you without you

Without what you think

What you value

What you care about

What you need

Nothing

You're the blueprint
You're the mark
It's been yours from the very start

Change your thoughts and
Shape your reality
It's your world
You create it and watch it grow

Conquer Fear

Looking down through clear skies on the airplane

Seeing squares of green land made perfectly

Makes me think

One day I'll scratch sky diving off my bucket list

One day I'll feel the worst fear of my life

And I'll face my fear in that very moment

Feeling a sense of confidence and excitement

Feeling like I can do anything

Fear is a great emotion

But overcoming fear feels liberating

Learning that the world is a scary place,

one that you don't know

One that you can explore, learn, and see

It's more out there

The world doesn't stop with just you and me

your neighborhood, your city, your state, your country,

your continent, your earth,

Not even your universe 🌍

You wonder about gravity and how it even holds you up
You wonder about life and what it's really about
What life is really for
And why you were granted a life on earth
You think about dying and think it won't be so bad
We're supposed to die right

There has been plenty life before and after us
What makes life so important
What makes us want to hold on to life
What makes us afraid to die
We're supposed to die right

We are so afraid to die we forget to live

Forget that we won't be here forever

Forget that some lives are taken away too soon

Why let fear hold us back

Why let any emotion control us

If we can conquer fear, we can conquer anything

The greatest life is a

fear-conquering life

Life Worth Living

I realize I don't actually know what I want

I don't actually have an idea of what I want

I don't even know where I want to end up

All I know is I want to know who I am

I want to learn what I want

I want to be most of all happy

Most of all not to have to question anything in my life

To know what I deserve and actually strive for it

I know I want to see the world

I want to conquer all my fears

And never miss a breath-taking moment

Never miss a flower

Never miss a breeze

Never miss the beauty in a simple thing

Never miss the art of the world

The art of the people

The art of the trees in every season

Especially winter

When the trees are naked and beautiful

Especially in the Spring during cherry blossom season,

my favorite season

The season that reminds me life is short

and doesn't last forever

The season that reminds me to cherish every moment

Cherish every person

Cherish every lesson

Cherish everything I've ever learned,

seen, felt, heard, tasted, and smelled

Because it could all be taken away just like that

In a blink of an eye it all could be gone

The people you love and cherish can die

Any given second, at any given time

So, what are we rushing for

Why are we fighting life

Why spend our whole life fighting

when we can spend the rest of our lives living

Question of Life

I walk, and I walk, and I walk
Trying to find my way
It doesn't feel like I'll ever find it
It, what is it that I'm looking for
It, what is it
I'm not sure
Will I ever be

Nothing last forever
Life on earth is meant to end
We're worrying and stressing over nothing

Life isn't about you
You're merely a ripple in time
One person versus an infinite people
When you die
The world lives on
People are born
People die

You realize life is short

Shorter than it should be

So what's there to stress about

What's there to really worry about

It'll all be over soon

What will you do while you're here

What difference will you make

That's the question

The ultimate *question of life*

The Healer

Somehow, I always end up being everyone's secret good luck charm

It's like I don't even exist when it really matters

The secret good luck charm that everyone needs and love

But don't see

Don't see when it's important to be seen

Lord, why me?

Lord, why me?

Lord, why me?

I ask Him this daily.

Is my sole purpose on earth

to be the secret to everyone's sauce

be the secret that nobody saw

I'm sure it's not

but I always end up that way

That way nobody seen or heard me,

but they know I'm there

Like a thief in the night

But the opposite of a thief

The thing that brings you peace

The thing that everyone hopes will always be

But unfortunately, this secret won't last for long

There's two things that can happen

This secret will never be learned and disappear

Or this secret will be heard even if it's your greatest fear

Even if the whole world knows you have a good luck charm

That you probably need

That's been pushing you behind your back which is the

reason why no one sees

Not even you sometimes even though you feel me

Even though I always show you the real me

The Healer, this is something I always will be

Crown

There she goes

Her wish had been granted

Managing to escape everything and everyone

Hoping someone

Comes after her

Saves her

Saves her from her living hell

Mental turmoil she takes herself through

The over-thinker just wanted to be through

Done with all the mistakes she's made

All the pain she felt

All the pain she caused herself

All the joy she might as well had been avoiding

On purpose

She hears a voice from above

Apologize to you

Don't be so hard on yourself

All the pain you felt and are feeling is good for the healing

For the love you long for

For the happier ever after you deserve

To be free

Free of pain

Free of all emotional bounds

Not walking around with her head hanging down

but with her head held
high

How else will her *crown*

align with the sky?

A Beautiful Woman

A beautiful woman

Who isn't afraid of her emotions

Who isn't afraid to say what she feels

And speak her truth

Whose voice is well used

A beautiful woman

Who isn't hard to understand

Because she'll explain to you time and time again

Until those times she can't waste her breathe

Until repeating herself drives her insane

Until she considers stooping to your level

But then she thinks again

A beautiful woman

Who isn't afraid to show love

Or kindness

Because she is love

And she is mindful

Always thinking of others before herself

Call her selfless

A beautiful woman

Who is selfless

But sometimes selfish

Because she realizes

She needs to be there for herself

A beautiful woman who is smart

Who expresses her emotions

Through art

A poet

Poetically spreading love

All over the world

I'm still me

The woman that wears her heart on her sleeve

On display for everyone to see

Not afraid of her hurt or pain

Because through it all, she remains

As sane as the naked eye can see

But deep down is where the pain runs deep

She still smiles because she knows it's not that bad

Even when she's sad

Emotions come as easily as they go

Why not let them show

She doesn't know

because she feels locked

Locked in a cage

Praying for God to take her pain away

Through her faith

She knows one day He will

And when He does

Her pain will turn into

peace

And she will do nothing

but drop to her knees

Giving God nothing but

the glory

Gratitude

Every day you wake up
You are blessed with a new day
A new chance to make a difference
A new chance to be kind
A new chance to reach your goals
A new chance to be a blessing

Imagine if you suffered from short-term memory loss
You can't remember the bad
You can't remember the pain
You can't remember the hurt
All you know is God allowed you to see another day
for a reason
And you make the most of it

Life is so, so beautiful
Life is not stress
Life is not worry
Life is not unhappiness
Every day is a blessing
That we don't have to be given
But we get it anyway

People that don't have much may be the happiest people
Because their happiness is not attached to things
But attached to life itself because
Life is so, so, so beautiful

Feel, Heal, Secure

It's not the feelings

It's the moments

The memories of those moments

The memory of how good it felt

Feeling that feeling

For that moment

A moment

In which we live

Because we're not promised the next

Because we're not promised tomorrow

So, we soar in our sorrows

And flow in our blessings

It's our time

It's the hour

It's the lesson

Memories are what shape us

Lessons are what make us

So we must soar

We must fly until we can't anymore

Feelings turn to living

Living turns to being

So be it

Part human, part spirit

How balanced are you?

We are human

Let us not forget that

Let us not forget that we have feelings we must feel

We have healing that we must will

We are human, but we are strong

We will always overcome

It's His will

Let's live for the triumphs and glory
Let's learn from our lessons
Let's rejoice in our blessings
Let's love instead of hate
Let love conquer our hearts
Let love conquer our minds
Let love conquer our spirits

Fear not for fear is what holds us back
Let go of the past
You've already gone through that
What did you learn?
What accountability did you take?
Nothing will change until we change ourselves
Nothing will change until we change our self-doubts

Switch that worry into worthiness

Switch that stress into sessions

of self-improvement

You must be resilient

You're going to have to feel it

Think of pain like every other emotion

Temporary

Non-lasting

Not forever

Live in the moment

Don't regret

Don't suppress

Feel, heal, secure

Secure what you've learned

What you've honed for the

journey on

Queen

Don't call me Queen and treat me like a piece of meat
Sexualizing my body but not stimulating my mind
Calling me Queen when you like the rest of these guys

See a Queen is a prized
possession if kindly
requested
and the effort is put in to
not be neglected
Being catered to and
loved
Given gifts just because
But know it's more than
materialistic to a Queen

Some guys may say she's mean
But that's because they're lazy
And don't wanna put in the work to get her
And most definitely not the work to keep her

A King is what she needs

A man who knows exactly what he needs

A man who isn't afraid of hard work for the Queen

He will

Please the queen

Praise the Queen

Love the Queen

All hail to the Queen

You know exactly what I mean

Not meant to be exaggerated

But let's just say you're getting educated

On how love for a Queen should be

Love a Queen the way a Queen should be loved

I promise

You're gonna get exactly what you deserve

all of the Queen

What an honor from Thee

Appreciate what you've worked for

What your heart hoped for

What you deserve plus more

Because a Queen knows how to give it

She can give it because she has it

She built herself from nothing

And turned it into everything

She earned that crown

Humbly understanding what God gave her

Gracefully bowing her head just to say "thank you"

He kisses her forehead and grabs her hand and kisses her
there

He tells her ...

Your legs don't have to be bruised from a bed
in a too little room

She presumes he means to be rude

But he lets her know it's the truth

She deserves more than she ever knew

More than she ever mentally consumed

She admits she's learning

Learning what her heart has been discerning

For a long while now

Wondering when she can finally let her guard down

Shit

She owes it to herself

It's herself she's been neglecting

It's herself she is hurting when she's hiding who she's really

meant to be

Everything is a Queen

There's no shame in her shine

She will in no way, shape, or form

dim her light

To feed the ego and cater to the insecurities of a man

This is not a part of God's plan

She prays every day to be lead and guided down the right

path

She trusts her intuition and follows her heart

She's been a Queen from the start

Ode to Mother Nature

The Universe Empowers Me

I saw three eagles
soaring in the sky
first thing this
morning
I imagined them being the three equal parts of me
Human, spirit, and soul
Soaring up above
In sequence
For a minute
At the right time
Signifying new beginnings

Meanwhile
Crickets roar in the background
Tingling sensations in my ears
Speaking from the Heavens
Mother Nature you

Mother Nature is incredible

In the Universe she flows

She grows

She lies

Like lions roaring

So loud the Heavens can hear

Are you listening, she's near

She's everywhere

She's in you

She's in me

She rises high in the sky

And sets at dusk

Sky pink and blue

To show a balance between me and you

Thank you, Lord for blessing us with the Universe

So magnificent

We see

We appreciate

We love

We cherish

We adore

Like the thunder we roar

Like the lightening we shine

Even the darkest skies

Deep, deep where darkness lies

We may find ourselves but

Like black butterflies

With magnificent designs

We fly

We flutter

We blow

We kiss those you want to bless with your love and your glow

Glow girl

You're golden

Glow girl

Your light is showing

Glow girl

Get on witcho "hoeing"

If that's what you wanna do

We're human beings and these double standards are

THREW!

Fallen Trees

Sometimes my emotions feel like fallen trees

Hopelessly wishing they don't stay with me

And find somewhere to be

But they lay there

Stuck

At the bottom of me

Until I cut them piece by piece

And pick them up and take them away

Hoping they're recycled positively

The feeling when nothing makes sense

Like fallen trees in a forest

You've lost your balance

You forgot to water yourself

You forgot to grow your roots

You forgot your roots can still be bruised

You forgot your roots need watering too

You lived on the surface level too long

All your hope is gone

Your pain stayed too long

You lived with it

You let it linger

Now it feels stuck

When you finally drop to your knees

You can use the wood of fallen trees as resources

To build a new you

Yes, you can be made anew

Today is a new day and tomorrow is too

Replant yourself
Ground back to your roots
And watch yourself grow
But this time build yourself a solid foundation
One that can't be ripped out, fall, or even chopped down
One so strong
You won't even
remember it was gone

Fallen trees are just a
reminder that your hope
was gone
But hope is renewable
Your soul is too
Never forget where you
came from
Never forget your roots

Lilies

A lily is planted during the winter and blooms during the fall

It lives through the harshest seasons

Reminds me of a strong, fierce woman

Struggling to make it through

but somehow still does

Even when she's in pain, she still loves

A lily represents humility, divinity, purity, and faithfulness

Reminds me of a woman who's humbly divine even if she's

not right for you

Leave her be if you don't see her beauty

She's faithful and pure

Her love sticks like morning dew

Her faith, loyalty, and love shines her way through

the darkest times

She's light even when the sun doesn't shine

A lily represents loveliness, hopefulness, and kindness

A lily is a constant reminder that kindness brings hope

And through hope prosperity, abundance and grace grows

A lily is a beauty and should be honored as such

So delicate to touch and easy to break but

A lily is protected from birth to demise

A lily teaches us to appreciate life

Butterfly Fly High

A butterfly, beautifully and
wonderfully made
Starts out crawling and ends
up flying
Represents the beauty of life

Represents the proof that
God wants us to know
He can turn nothing into
something
He can turn anything
beautiful through His love
and through His grace
All we must do is have patience and faith
Trust the process

Butterflies fluttering around giving us signs that You do exist
That we're on the right paths
That human and spirit can coexist
Flying around in pure bliss
Butterfly, your beauty may never be missed

Red Cardinal You

Red Cardinal you

So bright, red, and

true

You are you

You are unique

Your coat so shiny

It makes them think

It makes them wonder

How you made it over

Over the obstacles

Over the trials

But God saw you through

Everything happens for a reason

So, you must let go

You must flow

Flow with the divine

Your light must and will shine

You will lead them all

You will lead the way

Your love will not go astray

Your way is laid !!!

YOUR WAY IS MADE!

Birds and the Beauty of Early Spring Morning

Soft sun of early spring
You grace me with your
effeminacy

Nature putting on a show for me in twos and threes
Pairs of birds flying in harmony
Right above me
So magnificently

Your songs graces my entire being
Your ability to live in the moment
To fly around just for the enjoyment
Reminds us that aspiration can never be confused for strife

That I can live in harmony with ourselves and our goals

With the beauty of the moment

And the efficiency of our flow

The flow of life

The flow of not missing the enchantress of this site

Flying over my head playfully

Gracing me with your presence

Little black birds with fluffy orange spots on your wings

You've been there since the very beginning

Ducks are even swimming and flying around

in twos and threes

Quacking to the rhythm of my soul

Birds keep making the same loop over my head

We are one, our souls are aligned

Everything is perfect in this site

Ode to Patrice

Lonely

How can she ever be needy

She has all these things to fill her life

The lonely feelings comes when she lays awake at night

Or when she wishes she can call someone to vent

Forgetting her relationship with her higher self is the most

relevant

Her connection to the realm of the unseen

Fills her life

Fills her with light

Fills her when she lays awake at night

Fuels her through her morning strife

Affirmations

Prayers

Stretching and exercise

Create

Spread love and light

Make the moolah

Repeat

Random

Hi, my name is Patrice
When I'm bored, I write poetry
I am supposed to be sleep
but I'm up writing poetry
I have too many tattoos
I need to stop but I can't
My mind and my body is a work of art

Happy to be living in my purpose
the purpose that started before I hoped off the porch
Now I'm sitting here naked, fighting the urge to post naked
photos, post myself twerking, because eeehhhhh,
what would people think?

What image am I trying to display?
It's the image of being free
So, I'll be happy when I can completely break free

I'm taking every opportunity to express myself
I don't give a damn where I am
In the museum, on the street
It is what it is, so it be

You have all these clothes to fold and you sleepy
And all you wanna do is feed your mind
Patrice, take it easy
Connect with your higher self
She's dope right?

Sit with God's intuition

He shows you things

Things you would have never thought

He shows you your emotions

He shows you art

He shows you how to start

How to move

What to do

Where to go

He allows you to flow

Flow with the divine

Guiding you by His light

The light you show the world

Through your brand

Through your purpose

Through your mind

It's amazing right?

Yes!

It's like I've been missing this part of me and now it's so intriguing I can't even sleep

Journey to Self-Love

This was the last man she will let confuse lust for love in her
presence
She was looking for love in the wrong places
Ignoring her addiction
Was it an addiction to lust
An addiction to bust a nut
Or was it an addiction to the idea of love
Because she honestly made herself nut more than any man
ever

Her heart yearned loved
Her mind yearned for a distraction
A distraction from facing her fears
Living up to the idea
The idea of what she knew she was, is
Deep down in her heart
Past the fears
Past the distractions
To the idea of herself she had in her mind
To the self she can now show the world

Now that her heart is free

Not under lock and key

She unlocked the key to her soul

To the story that was never told

Through the pain she held on to because it felt normal

If she made it through the storm, through the hurt, through
the pain

She thought she could make it through again

But each time it got worst

Each time she was picking her heart from the dirt

Picking the specks from her self-worth

Picking right up where she left off

Looking for love in all the wrong places

Not seeing her own detrimental behavior

The pain she was causing herself

She understands now that pain has to be felt

Not avoided

Because if you avoid it

It will chase you

Chase you until you figure out the source

Until you dig your way through all the dirt

All the pain

All the yearning to just be you again

At the end there's real love

Love of God

Love you give yourself

Love that's never been felt

Because you were seeking it from somewhere else

When the source was God, the source was you

You were always the one who saw yourself through

With the help of God

Self-love is your best friend, your best man, your best woman

Your best you

Because through it all, *self-love will see you through*

Poet

It's like you're a poet, right?

Poets are supposed to hide

Be mysterious and secretive

Only give a little

A glimpse of themselves

But you're different

You're well-rounded

Multifaceted

You've been through some shit

You wear your scars proud

You sometimes act a clown

But that's okay

You boujie-ratchet

And there's nothing wrong with that

There's nothing wrong with any experiences you had

You actually regret none of it anymore

You're actually happy you got to experience the love

Even if it was "fake"

Even though nothing is real or fake

Nothing is everything, everything is nothing

Because we're not promised today

Or tomorrow

We're not promised any breath we take

So why stress or worry over things that aren't

A poet and a butterfly you say

A butterfly living freely

A poet expressing deeply

Thank You God

I've cracked the code

The code to life and all its strife

I count my blessings

I learn my lessons

The biggest lesson I've learned is to

"just be"

Nothing is everything and everything is nothing

We are one

Now I see

How you love others is how you love yourself internally

Ode To My Readers

Emotions

Do not be afraid of your emotions

That's how beauty is made

Beauty is made through hurt and pain

Your emotions make you a work of art

The art you have been from the very start

Emotions

Face them

Especially your fears

Fear is an emotion too

Fear makes you the opposite of you

Fear hides you from your true self

Emotions

Run after them until you run right through them

Until you get to the bliss and the beauty of it

The beauty of the other side

That fiery light that's waiting to shine

Emotions

Who you truly are on the inside

Grand Risings Kings and Queens

Remember, to just be

Don't forget we have feelings we must not obliterate

We have fear that we must investigate

We have healing that we must accommodate

We have our power to take back

We must secure what our hurt, pain, and fear is trying to

teach us

And instill into our souls

We must reject every lie that was ever told

Every lie that made us fold

Every time we broke our own hearts by giving too much of

ourselves

Just to feel like we belonged

Every time we forgot to hold ourselves and our love close to

our hearts

If you made it over the mountain

Through the woods

Into the light

Pat yourself on the back

You won

You will never be easily shook

Your love will be high on a pedestal

Waiting to be shared when the right person comes around

When the right person recognizes your crown

The crown that's always been there Kings and Queens

You will remind yourself every morning

When you say Grand Risings to yourself

Grand Risings to thee

Grand Risings Queens and the Kings

Note to Self:

I require the love that I give.

It's no longer a reciprocation that I'm longing.

It's ME I've been longing all along.

I love me!

1 Corinthian 13:4-13 "Love is patient, love is kind. It does not envy, it does not boast, it is not proud. It does not dishonor others, it is not self-seeking, it is not easily angered, it keeps no record of wrongs. Love does not delight in evil but rejoices with truth. It always protects, always trust, always preserves. Love never fails. But where there are prophecies, they will cease; where there are tongues, they will be stilled; where there is knowledge, it will pass away. For we know in part and we prophesy in part, but when completeness comes, what is in part disappears. When I was a child I talked like a child, I thought like a child, I reasoned like a child. When I became a man, I put the ways of childhood behind me. For now, we see only a reflection as in a mirror; then we shall see face to face. Now I know in part; then I shall know fully, even as I am fully known. And now these three remain: faith, hope and love. But the greatest of these is love." (NIV)

BIOAGRAPHY of Paradise's Storm

Self-love Activist, artist, poet, and writer, Patrice Brown a.k.a. Paradise's Storm, has dedicated the last four years of her life to a spiritual journey of self-love, emphasis on "of" because she believes that any journey is full of learning and is life-long. She wants others to know that we will all be learning until the day we transcend. Patrice focuses on feeling, healing, and securing what she learns for and passing the information on.

Patrice is Chicago native. She moved from her hometown, LeClaire Courts, to the northwest suburb area of Chicago at the age of 18. She lived there for four years to later move to the state of Maryland, where she has been the last seven years of her life. Living in multiple places has given her an open outlook on life and has increased her down-to-earth spirit.

Patrice dedicated six years of her life right after high school to obtain a bachelor's and a master's degree in business, management, and healthcare. Even though picking a major with a "monetary return" as suggested by other people directly after high school was a hard thing for her to do, she has always known that her purpose was to help people. Patrice knew that one day she wanted to own a business. She was blessed with a counselor that helped her understand that earning a degree in business will aid her in owning her own business as long as she keeps that in mind, and that healthcare will aid her in helping others no matter what kind of business she goes into. Today, Patrice uses her two degrees as the basis for her own business whose sole purpose is to help others heal. Patrice is a Certified Project Management Associate which aids her in starting and finishing projects within her own business.

Since Patrice was younger, she always felt a connection to her creative self. She wrote short stories and poetry, drew pictures, and played instruments as a child before "hoping off the porch". While in school Patrice tried to keep her entrepreneurship in mind, but she felt like her creative self was fading away. She made it through to the end, needing lots of mental rest but wanted to start something that will heal herself and in turn, heal others. She has engaged in a lot of spiritual research and took herself on a journey back to her creative self that she expresses through her brand, Modernly Ethnic. Ultimately, the time spent in college has given Patrice the basis she needs to start her own business and has led her to a healthy and knowledgeable life.

Creating this brand and being able to do all the creative things she did when she was younger, plus more, has given her a full sense of self and life. Patrice wrote her first book when she was 11 years old that is currently being rewritten and will be published by a world-renowned publisher, McClure Publishing, Inc.

Patrice plans to write books, create art, and be an activist of self-love until the day she transcends.

CPSIA information can be obtained
at www.ICGtesting.com
Printed in the USA
BVHW040936100521
606948BV00014B/419